The Art of

Staffing

2nd Edition

By

Steven D. Bradley, CPA, MBA

Contents

Who Should Read This Book

This book has been written for anyone working within the staffing industry, no matter how long they have been in their career or at what level position they currently hold. Many people in staffing do their jobs extremely well, but few understand the true ins and outs of a complex staffing organization. This book will explain how a staffing agency operates and what it takes to succeed during the ups and downs of business cycles.

It's also for any individual or business who uses staffing companies in their operations, whether for short term or long term needs. Understanding how a staffing company works will help your business better manage your staffing associates, your representatives, and the expectations of all parties. Once all expectations are fully understood and a common goal is set, you can practically guarantee a successful outcome. More than once, I have seen a disaster occur for all parties because they're not on the same page. In cases like these, there is more than enough blame to go around. Don't let this happen. Doing it right the first time will save time and money.

My Mentor

I never want to go to bed worrying about the IRS. – Kim Megonigal

I was very fortunate to have Kim Megonigal as my mentor. He founded and is CEO of Kimco Staffing Services Inc. and KimStaffHR Inc. (doing business as KTimeHR). Both companies are located in Irvine, California. Otherwise known as the "Permanent Temp Guy," Kim has spent his entire career in the staffing world.

His father before him, Tom Megonigal, a man whom I had the privilege to know and whom I respected greatly, was also a leader in the staffing industry.

I had the honor to work with Kim for thirteen years as CFO before my retirement. His knowledge, high ethics, and trust of his employees made his company a thirty-year-plus success. His insistence on doing what was right and legal, in conformance with proper accounting and tax law, and his views and fairness towards his competitors were a great inspiration to me.

I came to Kimco from the entertainment industry as a VP of finance and operations. Kim asked me to join his company to improve operations, optimize productivity, and increase profits. I truly thank him for his belief in me and his friendship. Tom, Kim's son has now taken the role of President of Kimco. Third generation in the staffing world.

Thank you, Kim, for what you have given me.
Friends always,
Steve

A special thanks to the best united team ever.
Chris Brady – Manager Risk, Safety and Contract review
Tammy Burton – Manager A/R and candidate compliance.
Jessica Fawcett – In-house Workers' Comp attorney
Richard Hayashi – Controller
Without these people my job would have been impossible to accomplish.
Thank You

About the Author

Steven D. Bradley received his bachelor of science in business with a concentration in accounting at California State University, Dominguez Hills. He then earned his MBA at Loyola Marymount University, with a focus on the behavioral science between levels of workers. During this time, he also passed the California CPA exam.

After working for Arthur Andersen and Associates, Steve operated his own accounting firm, providing audits, taxes and tax planning, and financial planning, before re-entering the private market with one of his clients. Holding a variety of management positions, in the late 1990s he landed at Pioneer Entertainment (a subsidiary of Pioneer Electronics) as VP of Finance and Operations. In 2005 he left Pioneer to become CFO of Kimco Staffing Services, CFO of KTimeHR (an ASO), and CFO of Keystone Insurance Company, a wholly owned captive insurance company. (All three were controlled under common ownership.) This was a dream position for him. Kim Megonigal, now semi-retired, left most of the management to his two presidents and Steve, with all three reporting directly to him.

In December 2017, Steve retired and started his next objective—the writing of this book.

Introduction

"There are more things in heaven and Earth, Horatio,
than are dreamt of in your philosophy."
– William Shakespeare, Hamlet

The staffing industry is an amazing vortex of business, relationships, negotiations, head-to-head conflicts with other staffing companies for the best clients, pricing, quality, quantity of available work force, ethics vs no ethics, legal vs questionable actions, and global conquest with your actions for the good of the company.

Yes, this may be a stretch for any staffing company, but your goal should be to compete in all of these arenas.

The Art of Staffing is so titled because I believe staffing is a true art, much like Leonardo Da Vinci painting the *Mona Lisa*, with every stroke of his brush describing a different lighting angle, from dark to light, in his masterpiece. You can look at it from the front and see one image, but move to the right and you'll see a different viewpoint. Move to the left again and you'll see something entirely different. An artist can paint a picture to allow you to see things in a variety of ways. Some will see the beauty of the image and some will see dark visions in the background. Neither view is entirely wrong nor right. In every painting by the great masters throughout the centuries, everyone sees a different perspective. Pablo Picasso painted abstracts that most could not understand, but that did not detract from the eye capturing views that amazed us all. Did they make sense to the average person? Probably not, but even today when you look at one, your eyes cannot absorb all it may demonstrate.

The title of this book, *The Art of Staffing*, was inspired by the late 6th century BCE book entitled *The Art of War*. Written by Sun Tzu over 2,500 years ago, this book taught about the actions and strategies needed to achieve success on the battlefield. I believe all business people should read *The Art of War*, as most of our military generals have, to attain a vision outside of the current business world. While that book may not directly relate to business as it is done today, it does reveal the strategic actions of visionary leaders who have become successful not just thousands of years ago but in business today.

In my humble version of that great book, you will learn the strategies to either become successful in the staffing industry or how to best work with staffing companies.

The Art of War insisted on your taking the high ground when going against a competitor. In those days the statement, "high ground," was literal. The army that held the higher ground was the one with the advantage. Spears traveled further and more efficiently when thrown in a downward trajectory, making the attack more to their advantage. And knowing what your enemy was doing was easier to discern from the high ground. The ability to see how your opponent was deploying their forces against you allowed you to move your forces to the locations needed to ensure your success.

For over 2,500 years this strategy has been used successfully; and for the staffing industry, nothing is more true today. Business can be viewed as war. There are winners and losers. You only hear about the winners, as the losers are lost to history. As in any conflict, the winners write the history books. It's the records of the winners we remember.

Things I Have Learned From Life

From the 1950 movie *Harvey,* starring Jimmy Stewart and Josephine Hull, I learned a lot about life and myself. For years on my desk I had a picture of Jimmy Stewart (Elwood) looking at a portrait of himself and Harvey, the 6' 3½" invisible rabbit that was an incarnation of a *pooka*, a benign but mischievous creature from Celtic mythology. When asked to mentor rising stars at the company, I always showed them this picture. It was a way to show them not to believe in how things are but what they could be if they believed in what that was possible. From this picture, I told them to believe that nothing was impossible, and to not just see things as they currently are but what they could be in the future.

There are things out there that no one can explain. Never say "never." See things that others cannot, and do not give up your ideals. You can make changes, even in the largest firms. Your smallest idea may change your company and the world.

In the movie, Jimmy Stewart says, "Years ago my mother used to say to me, she'd say, 'In this world, Elwood, you must be you must be oh so smart, or oh so pleasant.' Well, for years I was smart. I recommend pleasant. You may quote me."

This message was very true to me. For years as a CPA from a Big 8 accounting firm with an MBA from a major college, I thought I was hot stuff. But as I grew and matured, I was just like Elwood in the movie. Yes, maybe smarter than the average bear, but also looking for the opportunity to be pleasant. I found that as smart are you are, nothing can be achieved if you can't relate to the people who work with you and their problems.

Semi-retired now, I still have that picture of Jimmy Stewart and Harvey on my desk at home.

Your workers make things happen. Without them, leaders are nothing. Never forget that.

Ready? Let's get started!

1: A Brief History of Employee Staffing

Nothing ventured, nothing gained. – Benjamin Franklin

Some people in the staffing industry believe that employee staffing means placing workers to work at the location of the client in order to earn a profit for both their companies.

While that may be true, that is really just the end result of a much larger concept. The true concept of employee staffing is this:

To provide personnel needed to complete a project where existing resources are not available.

Employee staffing has always been around in one form or another. Over four thousand years ago the pharaohs built the pyramids using laborers that were not available in their own region. The pharaohs found their resources by conquering other regions and forcing the people to work under the direction of the pyramid architectures. It was all about providing a workforce to an area short of the needed resources to complete a project.

Now let us fast-forward to a more recent era, the eighteenth century where the same concept remained. Large landowners did not have enough people needed to work their fields. It is this time period that, tenant farming came into play. The landowner would allow the tenants to plant seeds, take care of the fields, and harvest the food. The landowner would then collect a percentage of the food grown by the people working the field. Through this example we move closer to staffing as we know it today, where in both parties benefit from the working arrangement. In many cases the landowner did not have the financial resources to hire the people to work the fields or the time to supervise the workers. This turned out to be a win-win for both parties. The workers did not need to be supervised, as they received nothing if they did not work hard and complete the task. Without the workers, the landowner would have land left fallow and unproductive.

In the first half of the twentieth century, workers would find an agency and pay the company a fee for finding them a company in need of their services. Rarely used today, but it does exist. This was more of a full-time type of job placement. In the second half of the century, the staffing industry started to provide what is now called temporary staffing. This provided manpower to a company in need of short-term requirements. Again, to complete a project where the company did not have the required resources.

Now let us move to the 1940s through the 1970s, when staffing really took off. To stay competitive and attract the best employees, many client companies had to provide benefits such as, vacation time off, sick leave, medical insurance, and company paid pension plans. The cost to employ a person was no longer just their wages and required taxes, it was all the extra costs needed to attract people to come work and retain them for years.

The cost to train a new person is quite expensive and time consuming. Plus, during this time, productivity of the new hire is lower than an experienced person. This is an important concept that many companies fail to understand. They value their employees as a necessary evil and pay them below market value, with the shortsighted strategy of replacing people who leave at the same low price. All smart companies realize this loss of productivity can seriously hurt the company and damage the bottom line.

During the above decades, as a longtime owner of a staffing company once told me, it was like having your own money-printing machine in your office. Huge profits were made even in a single-office company. Large companies started to realize it was cheaper to pay a staffing agency to provide manpower since the staffing companies rarely had to pay the additional premium costs as the client employer. Without the need for providing vacation time off, sick leave, medical insurance, and company paid pension plans, the staffing company could charge a large markup on the employee's base pay and still be cheaper than the large company that provided all the benefits.

Now let's move to the current time. There are staffing companies, both small and large, on almost every corner. Competition is extremely tough and hurtful for the overall industry. Temporary associates who used to work for one staffing agency are now listed at many agencies, and are able to pick and choose the best job for the most pay at whichever company offers the most. In many cases, staffing has become a commodity, like buying a battery at a store.

So why are there so many staffing companies? Because it's easy to start one. All you really need is a phone, some cash flow to fund the accounts receivable, and the ability to convince companies to use your service. In the direct hire world, you don't even need to have to outlay cash flow for temporary associates' payroll. You match the applicant to the client, applicant is hired and you bill the client.

Now let's look at what a staffing company provides to its clients.

2. What a Staffing Company Provides

You may delay, but time will not, and lost time is never found again. — Benjamin Franklin.

There are many types of staffing companies providing all kinds of workers: creative people, doctors, registered nurses and other medical professionals, and people in engineering, manufacturing, finance, technology, industrial, office, secretarial, and legal.

Each company has their own requirements and knowledge base that must be understood for the staffing company to be successful. You must know the language of the specific industry to communicate with the client effectively and to really understand the needs of the client to search for the people they are looking to hire. This is not as easy as one may think. To find the right person for the client, you have to get into the client's head to understand what they really need.

Most of the time, the company representative does not know exactly what they want; thus creating a problem. This makes it very difficult for the staffing agency to be successful.

All staffing companies will look for the client to provide a job description, education requirements, wage expected to pay, years of experience desired, and any specific skillset such as "must speak Spanish," "must know SAP," "must know tax law," etc.

There are many other factors that go into the finding the right person for the job. For the job seeker, there's one factor that cannot be written down on paper, and which is the most important ingredient: Does the person with whom you are interviewing *like* you?

On paper, you may be the perfect person for the job, but if there's no chemistry between you and the interviewer, you will not get the job. The old adage is true: People hire people they like.

This is not just true for hiring the applicant, but also for the company selecting a staffing agency. If the client representative does not like the staffing salesperson, no employment orders will be received.

There are a few basic types of employment opportunities provided by staffing agencies. They include temp-to-hire, temporary staffing (also in some cases called seasonal hiring), managed staffing, direct hire (also called permanent placement), and retained search.

Let's review them.

Temp-to Hire

Temp-to-hire is when the company has an opening they wish to fill, but they want to first try out the person to make sure they can do the job, fit in well with the environment of the company (do they like you?), and even simply show up on time. The temp-to-hire status can run from a couple of weeks to six months. At almost any time, the assignment can be ended if the employer finds the person is not the right person for that job, or if they find they really did not need to fill the position.

These kinds of associates are normally delivered through a branch location of the staffing company. During the trial time period, the staffing agency receives a *markup fee* above the base payroll amount. This markup fee covers employer taxes, workers' compensation expense, overhead costs, profit, and other costs that could be associated with the employment of the applicant.

This temporary worker remains an employee of the staffing agency until the client hires them and adds them to their own payroll. When the client makes the decision to hire the applicant as a fulltime employee, the client will pay a *conversion fee* (also known as liquidated damages) to the agency.

Everything should be negotiated before the applicant starts at the firm as a temp-to-hire. As an example, let's say the agreed-upon fee amount is 20% of the applicant's base annual salary. The applicant makes $25 per hour, so we multiply the $25/hour x 2,080 working hours in a year to give a result of $52,000 per year. The 20% conversion fee would be $10,400 (20% X $52,000).

However, typically, in the staffing agency agreement there's a declining payment schedule based on how long the applicant has worked for the client. An example may be:

Weeks worked:

1 to 2	20% fee
3 to 5	17% fee

6 to 8	15% fee
9 to 12	10% fee
13 to 16	5% fee
17 +	no fee

So if the temp-to-hire applicant worked 10 weeks before being hired full time, the client would pay the staffing company 10% (see chart) of the $52,000 or annual base salary or $5,200 in order to convert the applicant to an employee of their company.

The staffing agency can afford to do this because they have been earning a markup fee (margin) for the 10 weeks the applicant worked. In fact, many agencies calculate the reduction in fee percent directly based on the overhead and profit they made during the time the temp-to-hire applicant was on the agency's payroll while working for the client.

Regular Temporary Staffing

Regular temporary staffing is used when the client has a short-term need for additional manpower. This can be caused by vacations planned by their regular employees, sick leave, pregnancies where the employee may be out for a month or two, or just a short-term need for additional staff, such as for inventory counts. This can also be for longer term assignments where the client does not want to have the people on their payroll. This type of associate is normally delivered through a branch location of the staffing company. The longer-term associates may also be assigned by personnel of a managed staffing site (as described below).

As always, right person/right job is extremely important. Just putting a warm body on a job without taking all factors into consideration can be a major mistake. For example, if a client has an unqualified associate come into work to unload trucks, and that person gets hurt and needs workers' compensation, the resulting profits from that short-term assignment will never earn enough for the company to pay for the medical cost of the injury.

Another short-term staffing assignment is to hire people who have specific skills needed to complete a project where the talent needed is not already included in the client's regular workforce. Examples include a tax person, an accountant, or computer programmer. These skilled workers also allow the staffing agency to charge a higher per-hour pay rate and markup/profit for the company. Additionally, these jobs can often turn from a temporary assignment to a full-time position at the client. Thus, this assignment can create an unplanned conversion fee.

Managed Staffing (On-Site)

There are many forms of managed staffing. The most common is where a large company outsources some or all of the staff needed to fulfill the needs of the company for a specific task, such as warehousing operations. The client may keep the office staff and the warehouse supervisors on their payroll but outsource to the staffing company all remaining duties. These companies will have a large fixed fulltime "temporary" staff, and during a peak time period may increase the number of workers to meet their demand for resources.

On most managed staffing sites, the staffing agencies will have internal staff working fulltime exclusively at the client's location. All actions to attract applicants for that location are done within the location of that client. This includes advertising for the jobs, recruiting applicants, interviewing to assure the right person/right job concept, reviewing and completing all government forms (I-9s to ensure the people can legally work in the USA, W-4s for personal income tax deductions), hire and fire controls, timecards, and sometimes even the payroll processing.

They also deal directly with the management of the client and can attend safety meetings, production meetings, and manpower meetings. These people are the interface to assure that the proper number of headcount shows up on a daily basis and that the work is meeting the expectations of the client. This is a very important part of their job.

Internal staffing management of a managed staffing client can be a very difficult assignment. The pressure can be huge and the hours, especially during peak season, can be very long. The staffing manager has to make many assumptions based on the information readily available at the time and react to changes as conditions vary. The agency has to monitor the staffing managers, as the workload can be overwhelming and can result in burnout of the internal staff.

One major advantage for the agency in managed staffing is that there is little need for renting a location to perform the services, as the client normally provides the space, utilities, and computer lines for the onsite management. Many times, other costly items are also provided by the client, allowing the agency to provide a lower markup on the payroll dollars compared to the cost of running a branch operation. These tend to be larger assignments, and since a lot of the working associates may reach the tax limits, they can be much more profitable toward the end of the year. We will cover more about this later.

Additionally, if your actions build trust with the client, managed staffing clients can be with the staffing agencies for decades. In the first four months or so, the agency probably will not show a profit and will most likely see a negative cash flow due to higher employer taxes. This is because the temporary associates have not hit their tax limits. This varies from state to state. In California, for example, there is currently a total payroll tax that equals 9.2% of payroll (SUTA 6.2% and FUTA at 3.0%) for gross wages up to the first $7,000 per year. For a person making $11.00 per hour working 40 hours per week, it would take almost 16 weeks or 4 months before any staffing associate would reach the $7,000 gross wages limit. Once that limit is achieved, that employee becomes quite profitable.

That stable work force is what you depend on for the 3rd and 4th quarters to be profitable for the year. If there is high turnover and very few reach the limits for taxes, the account may not even break even at year's end. Remember, the company still has to pay their internal staff, even if the account is losing money.

If the client follows the retail business cycle, most of the work will be done in the second half of the year. Under this scenario, the temporary associate headcount will increase dramatically starting in the August time frame. For a client that has 800 temporary associates year round, they may well increase to 1,600 associates or more in the last half of the year, then decrease back to 800 after January.

It sounds great to double the business! Clients think the profit must be rolling in for the staffing agency, but in fact that's not the case. Since you've doubled the headcount, your costs will increase due to the need for additional internal staff resources to recruit and manage the additional associates. For every 100 associates added, you can expect your internal resources to increase by at least one person at the client, and additional headcount at your supporting headquarters. Plus, remember most of the additional 800 associates will barely, if at all, reach their state tax limits. You basically may make little to no money on the new hires in the second half of the year.

In those states that have high SUTA dollar limits, where the associate may never reach the tax limits, the account must be bid at a rate to still earn a profit. If a state has a SUTA limit of, say, $30,000, then it won't make a difference as to when the associates are hired, since the people who start on day one of the year may not reach the limit to stop the state taxes.

So why are staffing agencies trying to obtain managed staffing sites? Simply because the clients help cover the corporate costs that will be there, whether or not the client is there. (We will cover this later in the discussion of non-variable costs.) If you win the bid, you may be able to transfer the existing temporary associates of the prior staffing agency to your company, which greatly reduces the recruiting costs. It is also possible that the current onsite managers can be hired to retain the management team. The managers at these locations may lose their jobs if their current company loses the client. It makes sense, if the people are good, for the new staffing agency to try to hire and maintain the current internal management. There are many benefits to all parties. Due to the lack of training curve for the existing on-floor management, the bottom line on the income statement will benefit.

I have seen times where we've won the contract and the losing staffing company had no regard for the client. They moved the onsite management and transferred their staffing associates to another company they still had under contract. I do not agree with this tactic. What goes around comes around. Once you burn a bridge with this kind of action, you will never get that client back, even if the new provider fails. Yes, integrity matters.

I have seen time and time again that an inferior staffing agency won a RFP (request for proposal) due to low pricing. In a very short period of time, the client came back realizing the mistake they had made. Yes, it's hard for the management of a company to admit their actions were wrong; but to make their company a better place, they will often admit the error and make the correction.

Direct Hire

Direct hire, or so-called permanent placement, should be the most profitable department in the company. In this sell, the agency is providing the client access to people they would like to hire full-time from the start.

Since the agency receives no margin putting the person directly to work, they instead will receive a commission for finding the right person for the client. The commission is normally based on the basis salary for the first 12 months of salary. So if a person accepts a position at $100,000 per year and the agreed upon commission is 20%, the agency would receive a fee of $20,000. I have seen commissions as high as 40% and as low as 10%, depending on the volume and the difficulty of finding the right person. Compared to the temporary side, where you have worker's compensation expense, taxes, I-9s, W-4s, and the risk of employment lawsuits, this is a highly profitable transaction.

Since the agency has not had to make payroll, pay taxes, and carry the accounts receivable on their books (which is a real risk since you can lose the money you have already paid out), the risk of loss greatly diminishes.

However, particularly for a larger staffing agency, direct hire runs directly with the economy. When the need for employment resources is high (i.e., a low unemployment rate), direct hire should make a substantial profit. It's difficult to find good qualified people to work on a temporary assignment when they can find full-time positions with full benefits, vacation pay, 401k, sick leave, and bonuses. So the best option is to find fulltime work for the applicant for a direct hire fee.

On the other hand, when the cycle changes and no one is hiring, such as during a recession, employers do not want to take the risk of hiring a fulltime employee, even if the position must be filled. Plus, they don't want to pay a fee to hire a person when they have 100 resumes on their desk for every position available. In the 2008 Great Recession, we saw direct hire fees drop 80% in one year. If your business had been primarily based on the high-profit direct hire model, you could be out of business in a very short time.

The largest concern on direct hire is a counteroffer from the applicant's current employer. In many cases, if the person is exceptional, the employer will not accept their resignation, but make a counteroffer to retain their services. This is a hard situation for the employee. They may have been with the company for many years, have step ladder investing in their 401K plan, and may be losing their year-end bonus or profit sharing. So they will make the most of the decision based on what they believe is best for them at the time. In the past few years we've lost many fees due to this exact transaction. It's hard when your client is offering 25% more than the employee is currently paid and the existing employer matches or betters that offer. More often than not you will lose to the current employee.

So it's really better for a staffing company to have a mixture of both temporary staffing and direct hire. The temporary staffing side should pay the bills and keep the company open, and the direct hire side should be close to pure profit. If you can achieve this, you can have a company that can grow and survive the ups and downs of the economy.

Direct Hire, Retained Search

There is another format of direct hire—retained search. Under this agreement, the client agrees to pay your agency a fee for trying to find the perfect person. The retained fee arrangement is normally arranged with well-established employment agencies with a reputation for hiring top candidates with a proven track record for success.

In this form, the client agrees to pay around the same as a direct hire fee, but the fee is guaranteed whether you find the right person or not. (Of course, they expect you to find the right person!) Depending on the qualifications they need for the position, it may be a state-wide, country-wide, or international search. These are always high-end profile searches. Salary ranges can be $300,000 to $10 million per year or more. These searches are not a quick turnaround. It may take a year or more to find the right match.

The fee is not normally paid up front, but you can be looking at a very large fee if you find the perfect candidate.

Normally a percentage of the agreed upon fee (say 30% of the total fee) is earned when you have found several potential candidates.

The next step is to arrange interviews for the client with the candidates, provide background checks, check references, and provide any other client required information. At this point another 40% of the total fee is earned.

The last step is to find the candidate they believe is the right person. Now the full fee has been earned. The offer is made and hopefully it's accepted! You never really know how this is going to go. You did your best, but as with many things in life, that may not be good enough. It is not always a happy ending. I have seen this too many times to discuss. After all this, even after acceptance by the applicant, counteroffers can be made, and you may well lose the applicant. Then, if you want to retain the client, you may have to start over at no additional fee. This is true for retained search as well as regular direct hire placements.

Vendor Management Systems (VMS)

The VMS process has grown greatly over the past 20 years. Under the concept of VMS, the client hires an outside company to manage the hiring of the temporary associates using third-party staffing companies. They provide consolidated reports maybe by state, country, or worldwide. This may include multiple client requests including how many open orders exist, rate of fill, time to fill, and hours and costs to the client.

The VMS invoices the client directly. (The client may receive one invoice for all staffing worldwide.) As payment for their services, the VMS charges a percentage of gross amount invoiced to the client. The VMS bills the client directly based on hours worked and the pay rate plus the markup.

The staffing company does not need to send an invoice to the VMS. The staffing associates input their hours directly into the VMS system, which creates the invoice. The VMS pays the staffing companies based on the information provided. When the VMS is paid (say, 30 days after invoice date), the VMS has a week or so to pay the staffing agency. Since the staffing agency has to pay their employees (normally) weekly, the staffing agency has to pay the wages and taxes around 50 days before the staffing agency itself gets paid. This can be a major cash flow problem. Staffing agencies are not buying a product to provide to the client. If they were, they could slow down the payment to their other vendors until they got paid. In staffing this is not the case. The agency has to pay their associates weekly, and in most cases the related taxes on the next business day.

There was a major VMS disaster a few years ago. A major VMS for the entertainment industry filed bankruptcy and could not pay their taxes or the final payroll for the thousands of people they had working. This was true even though they required a deposit from the studios to insure payment for services rendered. There are a lot of questions as to where all the money went, but it was not there to pay the company's obligations. Since most staffing companies had equal to 50 days on accounts receivable, many large staffing companies and studios lost millions.

Let's look at the cost factor of the VMS concept. The client normally pays nothing for the use of their services. They receive a value due to the fact they only have to deal with one vendor, and that vendor can find staffing resources from many staffing companies.

The cost to the staffing agency can be very large. Take as an example an associate paid $15 per hour. They work 40 hours a week and the markup up is 35%. The VMS charges 5% fee for their services. So the weekly pay is $600 ($15 per hour times 40 hours). The markup is 35% and $600 (from above) x the markup is $210. Thus the weekly invoice is $810 (the $600 plus the markup of $210). The VMS charge is applied on the full invoice amount of $810. Thus a 5% VMS fee of the $810 invoice equals $40.50. (Plus, if they pay within 15 days of the point they received payment, the VMS will also normally take an early pay deduction of another 2%.)

Not taking the early pay discount into effect, the $40.50 they deduct from the amount they pay the staffing agency represents a reduction in original markup of 6.75% ((($810-40.50)/$600) - 1) = 28.25%, as opposed to 35%. So in reality, the true markup is not 35% but 28.25% (35% less the VMS fee of 6.75%). This a major cost of doing business with a VMS. Not only is your markup and profit greatly reduced, the staffing agency still has the accounts receivable risk on the books. Obviously the VMA fee has to be taken into consideration when bidding the project, but many companies do not know the real cost and may miss it in the bidding process.

If possible, I do not recommend doing business with a VMS, unless you have no other choice. The VMS is the only contact point with the client, and as a result, ideas to possibly improve safety or the process will never be heard by the client. The risk can be high and the profit can be lower. Of course if you are trying to just cover corporate costs with no expected true profit, it may be worth the risk.

3. Departments Within the Staffing Company

Most staffing companies have a set of common departments within the business. The size of the company will determine how many people are required and how many of the possible departments are needed.

All must have some kind of accounting department which includes general accounting, financial analysis, accounts payable (A/P), accounts receivable (A/R), payroll, and credit review.

Other departments include sales, IT, legal, human resources, candidate compliance, marketing, risk management, workers' compensation, branch personnel including recruiters, and facilities.

The C-suite management possibilities include the president, chief financial officer (CFO), chief executive officer (CEO—the top position), chief operations officer (COO), and chief information officer (CIO).

Throughout this book I will touch on many, but not all, of these departments and their importance to the organization.

Accounting

This is a must for any staffing company of any size. The function of an accounting department really does not change from industry to industry. All companies must close their books, normally on a monthly basis. This is extremely important since it tells management whether or not they are making a profit. It also can show the cash flow of the company to demonstrate if the company can remain operating and pay their bills.

All the accounting departments are important. If you don't pay your temporary associates (payroll department), they will walk out and find another company. If you don't pay your rent from the A/P area, the landlord will evict you. If you don't invoice your clients, they will not pay and you will quickly run out of cash.

Much goes on in the accounting department that few will ever have the opportunity to view. The accounting area also maintains the insurance requirements of the company, banking relationships, and advises the C-suite members of both historical information and projections of the near and long-term. While the CFO may not have the last say, he or she is the one closest to the financial results and should be taken very seriously.

Marketing

There is a lot of discussion regarding the effectiveness of marketing in the staffing industry. For most companies in the US, marketing is necessary to get your product and your brand in to the public arena. You could say that marketing sells most products.

However, this may not be the case for staffing. A lot of the business a large staffing agency receives is treated as a commodity and is extremely price sensitive, thus leaving few funds for marketing costs. As in any company, trying to determine the return on investment (ROI) is extremely difficult. In the staffing world, I have found it almost impossible.

There have been some exceptional staffing radio advertisements. The best I have heard was from Accountemps, a division of Robert Half, Inc. Who out there would not hire "Bob" the accountant? The "Bob" advertisements were brilliantly marketed, entertaining, and humorous.

There are many types of consumer-facing marketing strategies. For example:

Suites at a sporting/music arena. Very expensive, but can attract new clients and retain existing clients. I have found them to be very effective.

TV ads. Very expensive and must be run many times to be effective. I don't think I have ever seen a TV ad for any staffing company.

Radio. Cheaper than TV, but still costly, and the ad must be ran for an extended time period (i.e., three months) to be effective. I have seen a few companies using radio, but they are normally much larger firms aimed at selected industries, like accounting needs. This type of position demands a higher mark-up and gross margin, which may justify the marketing costs. They are normally directed at businesses and run during drive times.

Print advertising. This is still the most common form of advertising. Much cheaper than the above three. Again, aimed at businesses, they normally run in business journals and business newspapers. Print advertising is most often used for branding your company, not for specific jobs or positions.

Booths at conferences. I have found this as a great place to make contacts with all types of companies—some as vendors and some to provide additional sells. This also allows you an opportunity to show your brand. However, I have found it difficult to justify the cost due to low ROI.

Job fairs. These are a mixed goal function. Normally inexpensive, they give you the opportunity to both brand your company name and recruit new associates at the same time. Not all job fairs are created equally. Before signing up, you must do your homework as to the type of associates who will be attending and the type of businesses that will be attracted.

But the best marketing I have seen is the ability for a salesperson to hand brochures to a prospective client and build a relationship with the hiring person at the company. There is cost to this also—it's fairly expensive to hire and maintain salespeople. Even if you do have salespeople, you have must have something to sell that differentiates your company from the others.

There are two trains of thought here. Some staffing agencies have no sales people at all. They rely on telemarketers, or computer generated emails, or job search functions. Again, the ROI is hard to compute. The second train of thought is to upfront the cost to hire and maintain salespeople.

Sales Department

As mentioned above, good salespeople are hard to find and harder to keep. Top salespeople are always being recruited by other companies. Great salespeople make top dollar for both the company and themselves. It is not unusual for a top salesperson to earn an income from the low- to mid-six figures.

There are many different types of salespeople. At the branch level, there may be a person that handles transactional business. This type of business is normally to send one to ten associates to a specific client for a specific time period. The recruiter at the branches can also be a salesperson in these types of engagements. The larger accounts are normally not at the branch level. A director or VP of sales may be responsible for both finding the clients and staying closely involved with the maintenance of the client on a long-term basis—perhaps even decades.

Risk Management Department

One of the most valuable and overlooked corporate departments is the risk management organization. This department handles all insurance-related transactions including general liability, car insurance, workers' compensation, errors and omission, property, fire and earthquake insurance.

Normally, the safety team and client risk evaluators report to this department. Safety of a client is a key for making the assignment profitable. One error made by an associate in the safety arena can cost the agency millions of dollars. The risk evaluators should visit all larger clients on a regular basis, and sometimes daily. They should be sure that the work being performed at the client is consistent with the work agreed upon at the time of the agreement. If the actions have changed and the work has become more hazardous, the engagement should be reviewed by management for possible rate increases or exiting from the client.

The safety team must work with the client's own safety department. If they fail to do this, different messages can be delivered to the temporary work force, and costly accidents will occur.

On a regular basis, the safety team must perform a walk-through of the client's facility and must document any concerns regarding safety. This information, if there are concerns, must be brought to the staffing company's management and, if need be, the management of the client.

Safety is a team effort by both the client and the agency. The last thing any company, staffing or client, wants is to have a serious accident. The first rule of safety is to always want your employees to safely return home after work. A poor safety environment brings potential lawsuit and very expensive (maybe hundreds of thousands of dollars) OSHA fines to both parties. It just makes sense that safety is the top priority on any job.

Recruiters: Hunters vs Gatherers

These terms are normally related to the recruiters of the staffing agencies. Not all recruiters are the same, and depending on what your staffing agency is trying to

45

accomplish, could require completely different personalities. Just as in the olden days, real hunters left their communities to truly hunt and bring back food for the community. Gatherers, on the other hand, were more like farmers who stayed close to the community and brought back items they could find, like berries, fruits, nuts, etc. Again very different personalities.

Hunters are recruiters that go out searching for new clients or associates. They show a type of hunger that nothing is going to stop them. The hunter personality is one who searches for or seeks to achieve a goal. They tend to be outgoing, fearless, even to the point of being aggressive (sometimes too much). A hunter is needed either in the case of lower unemployment where there are few people looking for work (in which case the recruiter must hunt down people to employ and convince them to come work as an associate for the firm), or in a downturn economy where there are a lot of unemployed people and few clients are hiring (as in the Great Recession of 2008). During the recession, retail transactional staffing business all but dried up. Very few smaller clients were hiring staffing agencies. Most were cutting back on their own staff, just trying to stay in business with no need for additional workers. In this environment, hunters were very much in demand.

Gatherers (also sometimes called order takers) are recruiters who wait for the order or associates to come to them. Please understand, I'm not saying there's anything wrong with being a gatherer. It's simply a different need during a specific time period. If a large client needs 100 people and there are sufficient people looking for work, a mere ad on Craigslist may provide 300 people looking for jobs. The gatherer did not go looking for the client, the client called due to a need for staffing. At this point the gatherer must process the applicants quickly, picking the right person for the right job. Again, the gatherer did not go looking for the applicants (other than placing the ad)—the applicants called in looking for jobs.

The really hard part is this: During an economic cycle (say every seven years or so), you will need hunters part of the time and gatherers another part of the cycle. It's really difficult to turn a gatherer into a hunter and vice-versa. A top recruiter at one point in the cycle may be the worse recruiter at another point. The ability to adjust during the up and down times can be difficult. This has always been a problem in the staffing world.

4. How a Staffing Company Earns a Profit

Nothing is certain but death and taxes. – *Benjamin Franklin*

To keep its doors open, every business needs to earn a profit. Here's how staffing companies do it.

Markup

Most staffing companies add a markup percentage to the per hour rate the temporary associates are paid. This markup covers the employer's federal and state taxes, workers' compensation, benefits provided to the employee, overhead cost for the branch, overhead cost for any corporate identity, and hopefully a profit.

Let's say you have a 70% markup on a specific client. If the employee is paid $15 per hour, your staffing company would bill the client $15 x 70% = $10.50 plus the base per hour rate ($15) for a total bill rate of $25.50 per hour.

If by chance you have a client who wishes to pay a per-hour bill rate (some clients allow this), it's up to the staffing agency to find the right person at the lowest possible pay rate to maximize the staffing agency profit. Let's use the above example to illustrate this concept. The client comes to you and says "I will pay you $25.50 per hour to provide associates to perform the needed task". If you can find the right people at $15 per hour, your markup is 70%. This is calculated as follows: $25.50 bill rate/$15 pay rate = 1.70. Drop the 1, because the 1 is really the pay rate in the calculation. You end up with .70, which is 70%.

However, let's say the client offers you a bill rate of $25.50 per hour, but to find the right people, you have to pay $16 per hour to the associate. Using the same calculation in this paragraph, $25.50/16.00 = 1.59. Drop the 1 and your markup is 59%—much lower than the 70% markup in the prior example.

The staffing agency should be the expert on knowing the price per hour amount that's needed to obtain the right person. Say you know you can provide associates at $14 per hour. Same calculation is used, $25.50/$14.00 = 1.82, so the markup is 82%. Staffing agencies can use this to their advantage. Since no markup percentage is provided to the client, no pay rates are shown to the client. The client does not know what you are paying the people you send.

Since few companies outside the industry fully understand all the costs related to performing the staffing function, many just think all the 70% markup is going to profit. Nothing could be further from the truth. This 70% markup has to cover all the direct costs (employer taxes, workers' compensation, etc.) plus cover all the indirect costs like branch rent, utilities, general insurances, supplies, your own employees including recruiters, their employee taxes, and corporate costs.

Cash Flow

Many companies go out of business not because they aren't profitable but because they mishandled their cash flow. Of course, making a profit is necessary, but in order to survive all companies must have steady flow of cash to pay their employees and bills. The staffing industry is no different. The main difference for the staffing industry is that their "inventory" is their temporary associates workers.

These workers must be paid on each and every payday, and their related taxes must be paid shortly afterward. Failure to do either is a major problem. Workers who don't get paid, will not return to work the next day. Plus, the staffing industry is a fairly close family. Minutes after a staffing company can't make payroll, everyone knows about it, including the client. I have seen the transfer of employees to another staffing company, thus losing the client and the sales, happen as quickly as within a few hours of a missed payroll.

In most industries, you buy a product to resell, and then pay the supplier for the product in 30 to 45 days. This gives the company 30 to 45 days to sell the product and collect the money before the invoice for the product is due.

In the staffing industry, the company *must* pay their employees within a week after they have worked. But while the cash is going out to pay their employees, most clients have 30 to 60 day terms, so the incoming cash will not be received for a month or so. Depending on the size of the staffing company, this difference—call it the "float"—could be in the millions of dollars. For example, if a staffing agency has revenue of $150 million per year, they would need around $12 million in upfront cash flow to cover their accounts receivable.

The number one reason for a company to have to file for bankruptcy is cash flow problems. This is true for all types of companies. I have seen some staffing companies pay their employees but not pay their payroll taxes. This will work for a while, but the IRS does not take kindly to this practice. They will shut you down. The penalties and interest can double the amount you owe in a very short period of time. Do not do this.

In a staffing company that follows the retail industry, one that goes into peak during a specific time period, such as stores getting ready for back to school, Halloween and Christmas, the cash flow is even more important. A client may have 500 temporary associates year round and then increase to 1,000 for a few months. This is good for the staffing company, as you receive more sales and profit, but it requires double the cash flow for the time of peak. This is where a positive banking relationship is critical. Most companies can borrow money to get them through this time period, but the relationship with the bank must be established months before the need. Banks in the USA are very slow. It could take six months to establish a line of credit secured by the accounts receivable (A/R—the invoices not yet paid to your company) before a line can be established. And even then you normally can borrow 80% of your company's A/R. The remaining 20% is up to the company to make sure they can pay their bills. This is not an easy task, as banks are very careful to whom they lend money.

Revenue (Sales)

The top section of a profit and loss statement (P&L) is the amount you have invoiced the client, normally on a weekly basis. On a monthly basis these amounts are accumulated to show the revenue for the month. Many staffing companies are on a 4-4-5 week basis due to the fact that the invoicing is only done at the end of each week. A 4-4-5 week basis means the first month of the year has 4 weeks in the P&L, the second has 4 weeks, and the third has 5 weeks. Depending on the day that the year-end occurs, a year could have 52 or 53 weeks.

The temporary staffing revenue line on the P&L is simply the bill rate times the number of hours worked. If you had 10 associates working at $25.50 per hour and all worked 40 hours in the week, the sales (also called revenue) would be 10 x $25.50 x 40 hours = $10,200 for that week.

This temporary staffing sales calculation is standard throughout the industry.

The direct hire (also called permanent placement) is also included in the revenue section. Here some companies that record it differently. Since there is no related associate payroll or tax costs, most companies record the total direct hire fee as revenue with no related cost of sales. Thus 100% of the direct hire fee passes directly to the gross margin line. The only cost to the agency is the commission due to the recruiter for placing the applicant. Other agencies include the commission earned by the recruiter as part of cost of sales, so only the net fee will flow to the gross margin line.

Direct Costs (Cost of Sales)

Direct costs are those costs *directly resulting from the associate being on your payroll.* They are costs that would not be spent and would not show up on a profit and loss statement if the associate were not there. For example, the cost of the rent of your office is not a direct cost because you need to pay it regardless of what you pay your associates.

Wages

The largest of the direct costs consists of wages paid to the associates. This includes regular pay (also called straight time pay), which is the wages earned before considering overtime pay or double time pay. The states differ in this calculation. Some, including California, pay straight time, in most cases, for the first 8 hours worked in a day. The next 4 hours is overtime pay (say, 1.5 times straight time pay) and after 12 hours, would be paid double time.

Employer Taxes

The next highest expense in direct costs is normally employer-paid taxes. This is the tax burden the staffing agency has to pay to the federal and state governments. These taxes are on top of what the associates pay through deductions on their paychecks. In 2018, the federal government charges both the employee and the employer 6.2% of total wages until the employee wages exceeds $128,400. Most associates will not come close to reaching that wages amount. To reach that amount the employee would need to earn over $61 per hour and work full-time.

Another federal tax is Medicare. Both the employee and the employer must pay 1.45% on all wages earned, no matter how much the employee earns.

For most associates the payout to the federal government in taxes is 7.65% of all wages earned (6.2% + 1.45%).

There is another federal tax, which is caused by the States borrowing money from the Federal government to pay state unemployment compensation. This tax is called FUTA, which is for Federal Unemployment Tax Act which charges .6% on the first $7,000 of payroll per employee. If a state has to borrow money from the federal government to pay state unemployment insurance to those who have lost their jobs, the federal government will charge an additional .3% on the first $7,000 earned. This tax will continue to grow at an additional .3% each year until the state has repaid the loan to the federal government. During the Great Recession, many states had to borrow the money. Since that time all have repaid the loan amount. As of 2017, California was the only state that had not repaid the loan back. For 2017, the rate for FUTA was 2.7% of wages, up to $7,000 in California. During 2018 California repaid the loan, but it took a decade to do so at rate of a billion dollars per year.

The next tax is the state unemployment insurance (SUTA). This tax will vary based on the number of employees who file and collect unemployment benefits. And from state to state the percentage of tax varies substantially, and the limit where the state stops requiring payment of the tax also varies from very low to very high. In order to bid a contract, you must know your state's requirements.

Workers' Compensation

Normally the third highest cost in the direct cost category, this is the amount paid by the employer either to an insurance agency or the state to pay for the medical expenses of an injured employee. This varies greatly by state and by type of work the employee is performing. Four states—Ohio, North Dakota, Washington and Wyoming—have what is called monopolistic, requiring coverage by a state designated program. Based on my experience, this is the most efficient form and the cheapest form of coverage. If there is an injury, the state steps in and controls almost everything. The other 46 states are different and greatly more expensive. To have this expense run in the 5% to 10% of total payroll is not unusual.

Almost every state workers' compensation program has what is called *exclusive remedy*. An injured party can collect only for time off where they did not get paid, medical expenses, additional training, and perhaps a long-term benefit based on the percentage of the pay that the employee may lose due to the long-term loss usage of a body part. In most cases, they may *not* sue the employer directly for the cause of the injury. They must file through the workers' compensation insurance policy. Punitive damages and pain and suffering are not taken into consideration on workers' compensation claims.

Once the claim is filed, it is the insurance company's responsibility to manage the claim and pay the bills until the person can return to work. This process is not all that expensive, in most cases, until and unless the injured party retains a lawyer. These lawyers work on a contingency basis.

They will receive a percentage of the total award earned by the injured party. The higher the award the more the lawyer will earn. I have seen cases that should cost $5,000 end up costing $50,000 after the lawyer is involved. This was due to excessive doctor visits, excessive medical tests, excessive transportation to the doctor, home care, etc. Remember, the lawyer gets a percentage of the total claim.

In addition to the employee's lawyer, your insurance company must provide a lawyer to defend the case. Although the insurance company pays their lawyers, the cost will be reflected in higher premium costs to your company.

Basically, the states with the most workers' compensation lawyers have the highest workers' comp rates and expenses. I spent thirteen years in charge of an internal workers' compensation department including lawyers, claims management, captive (wholly owned) insurance company, risk management, and the safety team. We paid all these people to help assist our injured employees and try to keep costs under control. Without a doubt, it was the most frustrating part of my position as CFO of Kim's five companies, representing over 50% of my time. Again I say, right person, right job. If you put a person to work who cannot physically perform the requirements of the job, or if the client has an unsafe work environment, it will cost you more than you can ever make with the client.

Types of Workers' Compensation Policies

As discussed before, most states require the employer to provide workers' compensation coverage. There are three basic types of coverage:

1) Fully insured. This is where the company purchases a policy to pay for all claims, be they medical costs, legal costs, loss of pay, handling the administrative function of processing, closing the claim, and hiring private investigators to identify fraud claims. The staffing agency pays a stated amount as agreed with the insurance company. This amount fully insures the agency for the year (in many states it's a percent of payroll). The amount can be adjusted at year's end due to more or less payroll than projected. The percentage paid is based on the type of work and risk the associate preforms. Example: for a clerical worker, the agency may pay $1.50 per $100 of payroll paid. For an industrial worker the agency may pay $10.00 per $100 of payroll paid.

2) High deductible policy. With this type of insurance, the employer pays a lower percentage to the insurance company, but assumes the risk to pay for the claims. Example: with a $100,000 per claim deductible policy, the staffing company may only pay 30% of the going workers' compensation rate to the insurance company, but the staffing agency has to pay each claim up to $100,000 per claim. From the example above for a clerical worker, the company may pay 30% of the $1.50 per $100 of payroll, or $.45 per hundred. There is a real advantage to this type of policy if the staffing agency can keep the number of claims low and have a small dollar pay out per claim. The staffing company is assuming a financial risk if they fail to keep their workers' compensation incurred costs low. Additionally, the insurance company may demand a bond or trust account for the amount that may be paid out during the life of the claims for that year, in case the agency cannot pay their debts.

3) Self-Insured. If the state allows it, the staffing company can provide workers' compensation completely on their own. If self-insured, the company pays nothing to an insurance company. They assume 100% of the risk and all costs related to the injured party. Like the high deductible policy, if they can keep the number of claims and the payouts small, the staffing agency can materially increase their profit. In most states, self-insured is not easy to qualify for the staffing agency. The government does get involved, and most require a bond, letter of credit, or substantial deposit to cover the state should the agency go out of business. Whether the agency is around or not, someone has to continue to pay the claims of the injured party.

There are advantages and disadvantages to all the above types of workers' compensation policies.

In a fully insured plan you know exactly how much you are going to pay, but it's usually the highest cost as insurance companies want to make sure they have the funds to pay the claims and still earn a profit. If by chance the insurance company does lose money, the agency can expect their cost to increase the next year.

In a high deductible policy, you're paying a lower premium to the insurance company, but you may pay out more in claims than a fully insured plan would have cost.

In a self-insured program, you take 100% of the risk. If the agency is not large enough to cover the costs, one big claim could bring the company down. This is high risk because if the injury is devastating, one claim could run into the millions of dollars.

As far as costs and comparing all the states, California is by far the most expensive. It is not even close to Connecticut, the 2nd worst state, regarding cost of treatment and settlement. The most expensive states are:

1) California
2) Connecticut
3) New Jersey
4) New York
5) Alaska
6) Oklahoma
7) Illinois
8) Vermont
9) Delaware
10) Louisiana

The least expensive six states are (in order):

1) Nevada
2) Massachusetts
3) Virginia
4) Arkansas

5) Indiana

6) North Dakota

So if you're looking to expand your territory or start a new company, I would recommend you stay out of the expensive states, especially California, and look at the cheapest six.

Revenue Tax (or Sales Tax)

Revenue tax is a state tax that applies a percentage to the total invoice amount (wages plus the markup). Only a few states have this tax, but it can be a very expensive cost. Let's say the state charges 6% (yes, this is a real number) on an invoice of $10,000. The revenue tax on this amount would be $600. This amount is normally shown at the bottom of the invoice, much like sales tax would show on a normal receipt.

Let's now say that the markup on this invoice is 50%, thus making the wages portion of the invoice $6,667. Again $6,667 wages times 1.50 (50% mark-up) equals $10,000. Now let's look at the $600 tax as a percentage of markup. $600 / $6,667 = 9.0%. So to make up for the revenue tax, you would have to add 9 points to the desired markup to yield the same gross margin dollars, or 59% total. As you can see, since the tax is on total invoice not on wages, it can be very expensive.

Other Direct Costs

Although the above represents over 95% of the direct costs, there are other costs like background tests and drug screening that can add to the total direct costs.

Summary of Direct Costs (Cost of Sales)

If you look at a managed staffing environment, these direct cost can normally add up to 85% to 92% of total sales. For these accounts, the staffing agency can have 8% to 15% of margin to pay the remaining costs of the company plus the profit (if any). The retail business (branch accounts) have a higher markup on payroll. For this side of the business the cost may range from 70% to 85% of sales. But in the retail side you have additional costs to incur, such as rent.

Gross Margin

Gross margin is what pays the bills and provides the profit. Although some staffing agencies calculate gross margin differently, the end results are very close to each other. Gross margin is the difference between the amount billed to the client and all the costs directly associated with the staffing associate (cost of sales).

Where Your Profit Margins Increase

Once the SUTA limit is met, your gross margin percentage and dollars will increase. In the chart on page 69 you will see in the first three columns the state, minimum starting wage for that state, and the gross wage dollar amount to hit the limit on the SUTA.

Column four is the number of months it takes for an employee to reach the maximum SUTA rate for each state. Also, in column four, where the number is more than 12, it means that at minimum wage, working 40 hours per week for 52 weeks, the employee will never reach the SUTA limit.

Column five is the maximum SUTA rate for each state. While the range for most states has a minimum and maximum SUTA rate, many staffing companies are at the maximum rate due the type of business and the high turnover of employees.

The last column is the additional margin percentage that will provide more profit for the staffing company, assuming a 50% mark-up over pay once the SUTA maximum has been reached. The formula for the last column is SUTA rate x pay rate / bill rate.

The minimum wage and the point where some state taxes are no longer paid by the employer is an extremely important factor to making money and providing the right pricing for any assignment. As you can see, the minimum wages vary substantially state by state. The reason why the minimum wage is so important is once the staffing employee earns the SUTA limit the SUTA tax drops to zero for that given employee.

On page 69 and 70 are the minimum wages as of January 1, 2019.

State	Minimum Wage	SUTA Limit	Months to Reach SUTA Limit	Max SUTA Rate *	Margin add once SUTA Limit is reached
Alabama	$7.25	$8,000	6.4	6.80%	4.5%
Alaska	$9.84	$39,900	23.6	5.40%	3.6%
Arizona	$11.00	$7,000	3.7	12.76%	8.5%
Arkansas	$9.25	$10,000	6.3	14.30%	9.5%
California	$12.00	$7,000	3.4	6.20%	4.1%
Colorado	$11.10	$13,100	6.9	8.15%	5.4%
Connecticut	$10.10	$15,000	8.6	6.80%	4.5%
Delaware	$9.25	$16,500	10.4	8.20%	5.5%
DC	$14.00	$9,000	3.7	7.00%	4.7%
Florida	$8.25	$7,000	4.9	5.40%	3.6%
Georgia	$5.15	$9,500	10.7	8.10%	5.4%
Hawaii	$10.10	$46,900	27.0	5.60%	3.7%
Idaho	$7.25	$40,000	32.1	5.40%	3.6%
Illinois	$8.25	$12,960	9.1	6.93%	4.6%
Indiana	$7.25	$9,500	7.6	7.40%	4.9%
Iwoa	$7.25	$30,600	24.5	7.50%	5.0%
Kansas	$7.25	$14,000	11.2	7.60%	5.1%
Kentucky	$7.25	$10,500	8.4	9.25%	6.2%
Louisiana	$7.25	$7,700	6.2	6.20%	4.1%
Maine	$11.00	$12,000	6.3	5.46%	3.6%
Maryland	$10.10	$8,500	4.9	7.50%	5.0%
Massachusetts	$12.00	$15,000	7.3	12.65%	8.4%
Michigan	$10.00	$9,000	5.2	10.30%	6.9%
Minnesota	$9.86	$34,000	20.0	9.10%	6.1%
Mississippi	$7.25	$14,000	11.2	5.60%	3.7%
Missouri	$8.60	$12,000	8.1	8.37%	5.6%
Montana	$8.50	$33,000	22.6	6.30%	4.2%
Nebraska	$9.00	$9,000	5.8	5.40%	3.6%
Nevada	$8.25	$31,200	22.0	5.40%	3.6%
New Hampshire	$7.25	$14,000	11.2	7.50%	5.0%
New Jersey	$8.85	$34,400	22.6	5.80%	3.9%

* Maxumim rate was not available as of pulbishing date.
  2018 rates were used. Little changes were expected.

State	Minimum Wage	SUTA Limit	Months to Reach SUTA Limit	Max SUTA Rate *	Margin add once SUTA Limit is reached
New Mexico	$7.50	$24,800	19.2	5.40%	3.6%
New York	$11.10	$11,400	6.0	8.30%	5.5%
North Carolina	$7.25	$24,300	19.5	5.76%	3.8%
North Dakota	$7.25	$36,400	29.2	10.74%	7.2%
Ohio	$8.55	$9,500	6.5	9.00%	6.0%
Oklahoma	$7.25	$18,100	14.5	5.50%	3.7%
Oregon	$11.25	$40,600	21.0	5.40%	3.6%
Pennsylvania	$7.25	$10,000	8.0	11.03%	7.4%
Rhode Island	$10.50	$23,600	13.1	9.49%	6.3%
South Carolina	$7.25	$14,000	11.2	5.46%	3.6%
South Dakota	$9.10	$15,000	9.6	9.35%	6.2%
Tennessee	$7.25	$7,000	5.6	10.00%	6.7%
Texas	$7.25	$9,000	7.2	6.46%	4.3%
Utah	$7.25	$35,300	28.3	7.10%	4.7%
Vermont	$10.78	$15,600	8.4	7.70%	5.1%
Virginia	$7.25	$8,000	6.4	6.21%	4.1%
Washington	$12.00	$49,800	24.1	7.73%	5.2%
West Virginia	$8.75	$12,000	8.0	8.50%	5.7%
Wisconsin	$7.25	$14,000	11.2	12.00%	8.0%
Wyoming	$5.15	$25,400	28.7	8.78%	5.9%

* Maxumim rate was not available as of pulbishing date.
   2018 rates were used. Little changes were expected.

Bottom Line Profit and Loss

We've gone over the top two sections of a P&L (profit and loss statement), sales (revenue) and direct costs (cost of sales). The difference between these two represents the gross margin dollars on the P&L.

Say the company has $50,000 a month in sales and $40,000 in total direct costs. The gross margin would be $10,000. This represents a 20% gross margin ($10,000 / $50,000 = 20%). It is this gross margin that must cover all the other business expenses before determining if the company is profitable or at a loss.

The expenses included below the gross margin line include:

• Internal staff gross wage payroll (both at the branch level and at the corporate level).

• Internal staff commissions and bonuses.

• Internal staff employer payroll taxes.

• Internal staff workers' compensation expense.

• Internal staff benefits including medical insurance, 401k plan, and all other benefits offered to the employees.

These costs are normally called *personnel expenses*. They are below the gross margin line because they are not direct costs related to the sales or the wages of the temporary associates. There are some companies that combine the branch wages and expenses as part of the gross margin, but they are few and far apart. I personally do not believe these expenses should be part of gross margin, as the expenses are there even if you don't have the sales and wages to cover the payroll. Of course, if the sales are not high enough, you would need to reduce internal staff to stay profitable.

Other general and administration costs as included below:

- Legal expenses
- Audit fees
- Software amortization (a non-cash item)
- Depreciation (a non-cash item)
- Rent expense
- Utilities
- Insurance (non-employee) like car, earthquake, directors' and omission, general liability, business interruption, and many others.
- Interest expenses
- Banking fees

- Supplies

- Property taxes

- Recruiting expenses (like indeed.com, careerbuilder.com, advertisements, job fairs, etc.)

- Bad debt expense (it does happen)

- Company income taxes.

At this point, once you have the gross margin and subtract all the expenses, you can see if the company has a profit or a loss. If it ends up as a loss, the company has two choices: add profitable sales or reduce the non-gross margin expenses. There is an axiom that says "sales cures all." I have always said, "profitable sales cures all." It's easy to sell dollar bills for 95 cents each. Your sales will go up, but your expenses will go up more.

Variable vs Non-Variable Costs

After you get through the gross margin section, there are *variable costs and non-variable costs.* This is the deciding point where you may take less markup business and still add profit to the bottom line.

Variable costs are those costs below the gross margin line that you can change quickly—for example, internal salaries and related internal payroll taxes along with related benefits (Medical insurance, 401k match, deferred compensation, internal education, vacation pay, holidays, etc.), most marketing costs, entertainment, travel, and others. These costs can be adjusted if need be in a very short time period.

Non-variable (fixed) costs are those that are normally consistent, do not change due to volume changes, and cannot be quickly adjusted. For example, lease payments (normally from three to five years), general liability insurance costs (annual), depreciation and amortization of purchased equipment or software agreements, leased equipment (i.e., anything on a long term rental or lease agreement), IT commitments, recruiting search function agreements (normally one year), interest expense (this may go up or down, but normally cannot be eliminated quickly), some legal costs, and others.

The reason I bring this up is the concept of the *break-even point*. In any business, once you have hit the break-even point, the cost of production per item drops. Once you have completely paid for the non-variable costs and have enough volume to pay for the variable costs, any additional business you receive will add additional profit on a direct dollar basis to the bottom line. Since the non-variable costs have already been paid for, that portion also becomes profit.

Say you have:

Sales of	$1,000,000
Direct costs of	($800,000)
Which leaves a gross margin of	$200,000

Again, this is the GM amount that has to pay for all costs (other than the temporary associates) including profit.

Variable costs are	($100,000)
Non-variable costs are	($ 50,000)
Profit would be	$ 50,000

($1,000,000 - $800,000 - $100,000 - $50,000 = $50,000)

Sales are	100%
Direct costs are	(80%)
Gross margin	20%
Variable costs are	(10%)
Non-variable costs	(5%)
Profit is	5%

Let us look at a new large contract. Bid the normal way you bid a contract, which would include all costs needed to fulfill the contract:

Sales are	100%
Direct costs are	(80%)
Gross margin	20%
Variable costs are	(10%)
Non-variable costs are	0%
Profit is	10%

Since the non-variable costs have already been fully paid for by the existing business, there is no additional cost to the organization. The profit at the bottom line goes from 5% to 10% for that contract, or more since many variable costs only move based on hitting certain volume numbers. For example, if a branch wins a new account but does not have to add additional staff, the sales cost per staff goes down.

This is why large manufacturers can offer large retailers better pricing under a different brand name for the same product. Once their non-variable costs are covered, any additional sales, even at a lower price, can add more profit to the manufacturer.

Paying Temporary Associates: Cash Cards or Direct Deposit vs Paychecks

The ability to offer pay cards or direct deposit vary from state to state.

What is a pay card? A pay card is a rechargeable debit card that can be used to purchase anything just like a credit card. They look just like a credit card. Using this type of card, the weekly net payroll can be automatically uploaded to the card as the form of legal payment to the employee. Only the net payroll goes on these cards and is the ownership of the employee. They can allow the money to accumulate over time or they can spend it as soon as the net payroll dollars are uploaded on payday.

This is *not* a credit card, as the employee can only make purchases if the money is on the card. Having a pay card does not require you to have a bank account. It is a self-contained unit.

Using pay cards or direct deposit, the employer does not need to mail paychecks, have the employees come to the branch to collect their checks, or deliver the check directly to the employee. The cost of creating a check, bank fees for processing each check, the envelope, the mailing stamp cost, stuffing the checks, etc. can add up to $2.00 per check. If you pay 10,000 associates per week, that cost represents $1,040,000 per year.

Most states allow you to upload their paystubs and even W-2s at year's end. The possibility of fraudulent checks drops to almost zero. Additionally, the bank reconciliation is easy, as there are no outstanding checks.

Using pay cards, or direct deposit, does affect the cash flow of the company. When you pay someone with a check, there is a time lag—the float—for the checks to clear the bank. When paying payroll, using a check, this time period is not normally very long, as employees typically need their cash very near to payday. But you may have three or four days of float, especially over a weekend or holiday. Using the pay card or direct deposit, the employees receive their payment on payday, thus no cash float.

Before pay cards, many lower-paid earners may not have had a bank account. The paychecks they received had to be cashed at a different location. In came the cash trucks. For a fee, these trucks would travel to working locations to cash the employees' check for hard green money. The fee to do this could be as large as 10% of their total net pay. So if an employee had net pay of $500, the check-cashing fee would be $50.

Under direct deposit (which goes directly into the employee's bank account) the bank does not normally charge the employee a fee, and under the cash card, neither employer nor employee are charged for the acceptance of the cash on the card. Most pay card companies allow one or two withdraws per week at no charge if used as a debit card and most do not charge a fee if you use the card as a credit card no matter how many times it is used. Using as a credit card is the better choice.

W-2 vs 1099 Form

A W-2 form indicates that a person was an employee of the company on a regular basis. It also shows how much tax the employee paid to the government, which was deducted from the employee's paycheck. W-2s are sent to the employee and the IRS.

Many companies try to hire workers as independent contractors. They are not considered employees even though the independent contractors may come to work full-time, stand next to the company's actual full-time employees, and do the same work. With contractors, the cost is less due the fact that the company does not have to pay payroll taxes, benefits (including medical, 401k, and profit sharing), or workers' compensation insurance. Overtime is paid at straight time rate, not time and a half as required in most states.

At the end of the year, independent contractors receive a 1099 form from the company, which is also sent to the IRS. This tells the contractor and the government how much was paid the person. In recent years there have been lawsuits over when a company must recognize a worker as a W-2 employee. The IRS has placed specific requirements as to who may be categorized as an independent contractor.

IRS 20-Point Independent Contractor Checklist

How do you determine if a contractor should be paid on a W-2 or a 1099? The IRS has established a 20-point checklist that can be used as a guideline in determining whether a worker can legally be paid on a 1099. This checklist helps determine who has the "right of control." Does the employer have control or the "right of control" over the individual's performance of the job and how the individual accomplishes the job? The greater the control exercised over the terms and conditions of employment, the greater the chance that the controlling entity will be held to be the employer. The right to control (not the act itself) determines the status as an independent contractor or employee. The 20-point checklist is only a guideline; it does not guarantee that a person is correctly classified. There is no one single homogenous definition of the term "employee." Most agencies and courts typically look to the totality of the circumstances and balance the factors to determine whether a worker is an employee.

Here are the 20 points:

1. Must the individual take instructions from your management staff regarding when, where, and how work is to be done?

2. Does the individual receive training from your company?

3. Is the success or continuation of your business somewhat dependent on the type of service provided by the individual?

4. Must the individual personally perform the contracted services?

5. Have you hired, supervised, or paid individuals to assist the worker in completing the project stated in the contract?

6. Is there a continuing relationship between your company and the individual?

7. Must the individual work set hours?

8. Is the individual required to work full time at your company?

9. Is the work performed on company premises?

10. Is the individual required to follow a set sequence or routine in the performance of his work?

11. Must the individual give you reports regarding his/her work?

12. Is the individual paid by the hour, week, or month?

13. Do you reimburse the individual for business/travel expenses?

14. Do you supply the individual with needed tools or materials?

15. Have you made a significant investment in facilities used by the individual to perform services?

16. Is the individual free from suffering a loss or realizing a profit based on his work?

17. Does the individual only perform services for your company?

18. Does the individual limit the availability of his services to the general public?

19. Do you have the right to discharge the individual?

20. May the individual terminate his services at any time?

In general, "no" answers to questions 1-16 and "yes" answers to questions 17-20 indicate an independent contractor. However, a simple majority of "no" answers to questions 1 to 16 and "yes" answers to questions 17 to 20 does not guarantee independent contractor treatment. Some questions are either irrelevant or of less importance because the answers may apply equally to employees and independent contractors.

While there is some (very little) gray area with the IRS, an employer must be very careful not to cross the line when making the decision to classify a worker as an independent contractor.

5. Best Practices

What goes around comes around. – Unknown

Vision for the Company

It really doesn't matter what the achievements of a company have been the in the past: What's important is to have a vision for the future. People who have a vision of the future are rare. Look at Steve Jobs, the co-founder of Apple. A visionary, yes, but also one of the best salesmen of all time. He knew that building a brand was just as important as the products they produced. The thought of a new Apple product was all he needed to send his followers into a frenzy. When the new iPhone was about to come out, he didn't need to tell the consumer what new features were included or what they were buying. He just told people the release date and they would stand in line to purchase the phone. The consumer knew what they were going to get was going to be exciting. Few entrepreneurs have been able to ask for a premium price for a product that the consumer has never seen before. He was a genius and a true visionary.

Bill Gates, co-founder of Microsoft, was another true visionary. He was offered a price to sell his company early on, but turned it down. His concept of licensing the product to the consumer instead of selling it was a game changer. This way he got to charge for updates and new releases. Companies have to pay annual licensing fees to keep the purchased product, thus creating a constant flow of cash to the seller for a product they had already bought. He too is, a genius and a true visionary.

Elon Musk, founder of Tesla, has never made an annual profit at Tesla. In fact, they lose hundreds of millions a year. But his vision has made Tesla one of the highest valued companies of all time. Yes, they make amazing products. He sells a vision of the future that people want to see. His ideas, are all over the place: Tesla, SpaceX, Neuralink (to develop an implantable brain-computer interface!), boring tunnels for high speed transportation, developing a mega-factory for battery manufacturing, and combining Solar City with Tesla, specializing in solar energy. He has the determination to put the right people in charge and the ability to sell people what they want for a better future.

While your company may not have the visionaries discussed above—very few do—the leaders of your company *must* have a vision to establish your company on a sound foundation while always innovating. You cannot remain in the status quo. The company that never changes will not survive. The leader has to stay in touch with what's going on in the current environment and have ideas as to where the industry is going. This is how a company advances for the future.

Relationships

In all forms of business, people prefer working with people they like, have common interests with, and can relate to their needs. This "warm and fuzzy" feeling is extremely important in connecting with a potential client. The relationship between the salesperson, the staffing agency managers, the recruiters, and the client will make or break the deal.

For this type of relationship, pricing is seen as a secondary action. I have seen clients leave one staffing company over pricing and within a month come back. Normally this is due to poor service and the lack of the new agency understanding the client's personnel needs.

Again, right person, right job.

Now I'm not saying that price does not matter, but I am saying the difference between 50% markup and 53% markup (or even a 55% markup) is rarely the deciding factor if a relationship exists. Where pricing does make a difference is when the decision of which agency to use is taken away from the actual client users (i.e., like floor managers). This is normally in a larger company where they use a procurement department, which *only* compares the pricing, to make the determination as to which agency to use. These procurement departments are rewarded only on how much they save without taking into consideration the end production results.

It's like the US government using only the lowest-priced option. It's concerning viewing a rocket blasting to the Moon, knowing the government used only the cheapest priced parts. It just doesn't give one a comfortable feeling. Additionally, which I have seen many times, when the government awards a contract to the lowest price vendor, the government pays a deposit to the vendor as part of the deal. The vendor takes the money and spends it on machinery, raw materials, and tooling, but fails to produce the needed government product. At this point the government has to go to an established vendor, at a higher price, and a pay premium for a rush charge to get the items on time.

From my experience, this is exactly what occurs when procurement departments are involved.

Many companies use several staffing agencies to fulfill their personnel orders. There are two types of companies that do this.

The first is a company that has a need for a specific hard-to-find candidate. For this company pricing is secondary. The agency that can quickly find the right person will fill the position, even at a higher price.

The second type of company is one where they don't want all their eggs in one basket. If one agency cannot find or process the quantity of associates needed by the client, then the client may have two agencies or more. An example of this is when the staffing company has grown too fast and can't handle the cash flow requirements. When this happens, the agency may not be able to make payroll and will lose all the associates working at that location. This would be a major hardship if the client used only one agency.

There are other types of bidding. One is the reverse auction concept. This is where the client contracts out to an auction house to find the cheapest company to do the work. Staffing agencies are asked to bid, via the internet, to provide workers based on a markup. There is a countdown and all bids must be made before the countdown reaches zero. They can bid many times, continuing to *reduce* their requested mark-up. The lowest markup wins. I have been through many of these reverse auctions. We never won one. To provide a quality program, the lowest price bidder almost never can deliver, at least not legally.

Another type of bidding is the request for proposal or RFP. Under this concept the client will send invitations for a few staffing agencies requesting them to complete a long detailed proposal to win their business. This type of bidding may start with ten or more staffing agencies. These proposals may be 40 to 100 pages long and ask for details of just about anything you can think of. There is a set timeline that the agencies must meet. The first round is completed by the client using the responses provided by the agencies. Once this is completed, the client may reduce the list of agencies still in the running to about three or four. At this point, the client will invite the remaining agencies to personally present their plans. From these presentations the client may select the finalists and request a best and final pricing opportunity. At the completion of this process the agency is selected. This RFP process does include the relationship factor. If the client has a good relationship with one of the finalists and all other factors are similar, the relationship factor normally will be the final decider.

Ethics in Staffing

Most staffing companies run their businesses legally and ethically. The company I came from was ethical to the nth degree. We literally refused tens of millions of dollars in business to maintain the ethics within the company. But there are some that search for a reason to gain an advantage over their competitors.

The most common area of questionable ethics is knowingly hiring undocumented workers. These are people who do not have the right to work in the USA legally. The staffing company knows that these workers will not normally cause problems because they don't want to bring attention to themselves. They want to keep their jobs since they are not assured of finding another one, and they don't want to be discovered and deported.

The next most common technique is miscoding workers' compensation codes, hoping the insurer won't find out. Listing a person as a clerical employee instead of a factory worker can save the agency 8% or more. In many cases the agency will bid the contract low to get it, but can only make a profit if they can pay the lower rate. Once the insurer figures out the correct code and charges the agency, the agency may not have the ability to remain in business. So they shut it down and start another one. Several people have ended up in jail doing this.

Another technique is paying workers in cash. No taxes, no workers' compensation, and no benefits are paid. This normally will get caught but it may take some time. Jail is possible.

The best policy is to run the business ethically and legally. It can be frustrating seeing other companies winning contracts that you should have won over pricing due to the other agency's lack of ethics. But you will sleep better and stay out of jail.

6. Structure of a Staffing Company

Money isn't the most important thing in life, but it doesn't hurt. – Unknown

Like any other organization, a staffing company can have one of several legal forms.

C Corporation

Most large companies are C corporations. This is a company that is really a stand-alone entity. Hundreds or thousands of shareholders invest in the company in hopes of increased value of the stock and/or dividend distributions. These companies normally have high cost of administration due to the requirements of the shareholders and the Securities and Exchange Commission (SEC), the government regulator of publicly held companies. For a C corporation to exist they must have annual board of directors meeting and, while not required, quarterly status meetings with the shareholders. All board of director's meetings must be legally recorded, which normally requires authorized representation.

They are also taxed differently than the other types of companies. Since they are true entities of their own they are taxed as an entity of its own by the IRS. Then any money (as in dividends) are taxed at the prevailing tax rate when distributed to the shareholders. This double taxation is a major reason why many companies decide not to use the C corporation status. The major advantage for a C corporation is that the legal liability in case of a lawsuit falls only on the company, not the people who invested in the company. This is a huge consideration when considering the type of company to set up. In a C-corporation, whatever you invest in the stock of the company is all you have to risk. By risk I mean, if you invest $10,000 or $100,000,000 dollars, you cannot lose more than the amount you invested. (Of course based on legal actions you never know).

Subchapter S Corporation

Still protected as if it was a C corporation from the legal status, this type of corporation passes the taxation of the S corporation directly to the shareholders. The earnings flow directly to the owners as ordinary income, rather than being taxed at the C corporation rate. Under this type of company, while still having the advantage of the legal status in case of lawsuits, it can transfer the income directly to the shareholders. You would still have the requirements of board of director minutes and board of director's meetings. As an S corporation, you can only have a limited number of shareholders, so the probability of going public is limited. The S corporation would have to convert to a C corporation before that would be possible.

LLC (as allowed in some states)

Let's now discuss the LLC (limited liability company). Under this type of company, much like the S corporation, liability is limited, but the requirements of the board of director's minutes and board of director's meetings, is eliminated. You should have meetings and document them, but the legal requirements are greatly diminished. (Please see your attorney if you any questions, I am a CPA, not a source for legal representation, for this any part of book).

Sole Proprietor and Partnership

Under these types of companies, which I do not recommend, you as an individual take on the responsibility of the work you are performing. If you make a mistake, you personally can be sued for whatever damages the courts award to a prevailing party. A representation letter can, on a limited basis, protect you, but in most cases not completely. Unless you have nothing to risk, like your house, 401k investments, stocks, or other assets, it may not harm you since few will sue if they can't receive anything. But for those who have something to risk, this is not the approach you should take.

7. Conclusion

The two most important things in life are time and energy, and if you are absent of either, you have nothing. – Unknown

The staffing industry has changed over the years, as must all that have a desire to survive. There is a real and growing market for this industry.

Staffing is one of the few businesses that can be started without a lot of up front capital. There is no inventory to be carried that requires a lot of upfront cash, but the company must be able to carry the accounts receivable to stay as an operating entity. As long as the company can make proper planning, with banks and great management, the growth factor is unlimited.

I have been told there is enough business so a war between staffing companies should not occur, but it does happen during time of recession. During this time everyone will undercut the current provider to cover the non-variable costs. Once this starts, it is a lose-lose situation for all staffing companies. Quite often, the client will use a low rate offer to reduce the markup rate with their current agency, thus reducing the profit to the agency. The client is the only one to win in this scenario.

My goal in writing this book was to provide an overall concept of the industry, both from the internal industry and the outside industry. Staffing is not rocket science, but you do need to be able to communicate as a businessperson. You will need to provide the client with the best people to achieve the goals of the company. Again, people hire people they like. This goes back to the "Harvey" concept. Both from the sales side of the staffing company and the associate side, there must be common respect. Right person, right job.

If you can do this, you will be successful!

8. Fifteen Questions

The purpose of this short exam is to check your understanding of the staffing concept. Please circle the correct answer before checking the answers, which can be found on page 105.

1) What is temp-to-hire?

A: A position that needs to be filled ASAP.

B: A short-term position that may extended for a month or more.

C: Temp-to-hire is when the company has a real opening they wish to fill, but want to try the person first.

D: All of the above.

2) What is regular temporary staffing?

A: All staffing is regular staffing.

B: A legal requirement as a position in the company.

C: When the client has a short-term need for additional personnel.

D: All of the above.

3) What is a managed staffing account?

A. All staffing is managed as part of the agreement with the client.

B. A company hires an outside staffing agency to manage the temporary associates.

C. Both A and B.

D. Neither A or B.

4) What is direct hire?

A. The company contracts with the staffing agency to hire a full-time person from the start.

B. The company hires its own temporary workers by putting ads on Craigslist.

C. A company would like to test the candidate before hiring.

D. None of the above.

5) What is a vendor management system (VMS)?

A. Same as an on-site.

B. The client hires an outside company to manage the staffing agencies in the hiring of the temporary associates.

C. It is a concept that never ends up working.

D. None of the above.

6) What is markup?

A. It is a set of changes made to a contract before signature.

B. It is amount added to the margin for billing purposes.

C. It is a percentage added to the per-hour rate the temporary associates are paid.

D. None of the above.

7) What is gross margin?

A. The difference between the amount billed to the client and the costs directly associated with the staffing associate.

B. It is what pays the expenses of the staffing agency.

C. Different staffing companies calculate it differently.

D. All of the above.

8) What taxes are part of direct costs associated with the staffing associate (COS)?

A. The taxes the employee pays.

B. The taxes the client pays.

C. The taxes the employer pays.

D. All of the above.

9) What is worker's compensation insurance expense?

A. It is the amount paid to the employee.

B. It is the amount a client pays for the temporary associate.

C. It is a form of insurance for an injured employee.

D. None of the above.

10) What is a variable cost?

A. A cost that will change due to volume.

B. A cost such as rent that will not change.

C. Both A and B.

D. Neither A or B.

11) What is an example of a non-variable cost?

A. Employer FICA tax.

B. Depreciation.

C. Wages paid to associates.

D. All of the above.

12) What is a break-even point?

A. The point where a company has enough gross margin to cover all other company costs.

B. It is a theoretical concept used in financial reviews.

C. It does not exist. Just a concept.

D. All the above.

13) What is an advantage of using a pay card?

A. It eliminates the need to cut checks to an employee.

B. It can save on postage.

C. It is easier to reconcile the bank account.

D. All the above.

14) You should have all employees on a Form 1099 basis rather than a W-2 because it is easier.

A. True

B. False

15) Why is the SUTA wage limit important?

A. Once an employee reaches the SUTA limit, all employer taxes are eliminated.

B. Once an employee reaches the SUTA limit, the gross margin for the company increases.

C. It is only valuable for managed staffing accounts

D. None of the above.

Answers to the 15 Questions

1) C. A temp-to-hire position is when an employer would like to try out an employee before hiring the person full time.

2) C. Regular temp assignments are normally short-term to provide additional personnel.

3) B. A managed staffing account is one where client hires an outside staffing agency to fully or mostly manage the temporary associates from start to finish.

4) A. Direct hire is when the client has an opening and requests that the staffing agency find the applicant for consideration. The client interviews, makes the hiring decision, and from day one is on the client's payroll.

5) B. A vendor management system (VMS) company receives a percentage of the gross billing from the staffing agencies for their service to the client in managing the staffing.

6) C. It is the percentage added above the pay rate. If the employee is paid $15 per hour, your staffing company would bill the client $15 x 50% markup = $7.50 plus

the base per hour rate ($15.00) for a total bill rate of $22.50 per hour.

7) D. All the above. In A, it is the sales (billing) minus the COS (direct costs associated with the staffing associate) equals gross margin. In B, gross margin is what pays all other costs of the company. In C, some companies do include or exclude other costs in direct costs.

8) C. Direct cost is part of COS. Gross wages are included as part of COS, but the employer has to pay additional federal taxes.

9) C. In most states, workers' compensation insurance is required to be paid by employer. This covers the cost for medical services among other costs for an injured employee.

10) A. Variable costs are those costs that change based on increasing or decreasing your temporary associates. Examples would be payroll taxes and workers' compensation. As wages go down, so would payroll taxes and workers' compensation expenses.

11) B. Depreciation is a non-variable cost, since the amount of expense on a monthly basis does not change if the business volume were to increase or decrease.

12) A. The break-even point is when you have enough revenues to cover all your costs. The bottom line of the profit and loss statement would show zero profit earned.

13) D. Pay cards can save a lot of money for the agency if done correctly. Each state may have their own requirements. Plus, as there are no checks written, there is no need for a bank reconciliation.

14) B. While having all employees on 1099s would be easy and cheaper, the IRS has strict qualifications that make it very difficult to have employees eligible to receive a 1099. Unless they are an outside vendor, you should stay away from 1099s.

15) B. Once the SUTA limit is met, the amount you pay to the state drops by the amount of the SUTA percent rate. SUTA is a state tax, and all federal and other taxes must continue to be paid unless they meet those tax limits. Medicare has no limit. Even if you made a

billion dollars on your W-2, you would still pay 1.45% on the whole amount.

www.ingramcontent.com/pod-product-compliance
Lightning Source LLC
Chambersburg PA
CBHW071207220526
45468CB00002B/534